praise for DEAR DIVINE Daughter

"As girls read *Dear Divine Daughter* and use the prompts inside, they will be able to more clearly see their divine potential and develop the characteristics needed to become their best selves."

—Elaine S. Dalton
Young Women General President of The Church of Jesus Christ of Latter-day Saints

"One million cheers for *Dear Divine Daughter*. When women see themselves in holy scripture, divinity is illuminated. And the world is blessed by this knowing."

—Ganel-Lyn Condie
Best-selling author, popular speaker, and video host

"Told sweetly and simply, these beautifully illustrated stories will capture your daughter's heart and open her eyes to the wide variety of women's stories in the scriptures. She, and probably you as well, will discover new heroines and role models that will last a lifetime!"

—Heather Farrell
Author of *Walking with the Women of the Old Testament* and the popular blog womeninthescriptures.com

"I love that this book about women is created by women & illustrated by women. Beautifully illustrated and colorful, I'm sure girls will be inspired by the stories of heroines from the Bible, some well-known, and some lesser known."

—Rose Datoc Dall
Contemporary figurative artist

"This book shows that strong or soft, bold or meek, all girls around the world can leverage their unique, God-given characteristics to make a difference for good!"

—McArthur Krishna
Coauthor of the *Girls Who Choose God* series

"With accessible fairytale-like retellings and thought-provoking questions, *Dear Divine Daughter* is a great tool for helping children engage with Bible stories."

—Sierra Wilson
Author of *Standout Saints*

"The stories and artwork in *Dear Divine Daughter* beautifully illustrate both the virtues and actions of the faithful, brave, and righteous women in the Bible. Girls will discover role models for today in the women who changed the world with their faith more than 2,000 years ago."

—Jodi Orgill Brown
Award-winning author of *The Sun Still Shines*, professional speaker, and brain tumor survivor

"This book brings to life many stories of faithful women told often in passing. The pictures draw you in and the words inspire. I love reading about these women and feel closer to Heavenly Father and more empowered to show up as one of his Divine Daughters. I can't wait to read every word with my daughter. This book will surely help me have conversations with her about her worth and her future. We're raising the next generation of faithful women and this book is a great guide."

—Michelle McCullough
Author and speaker

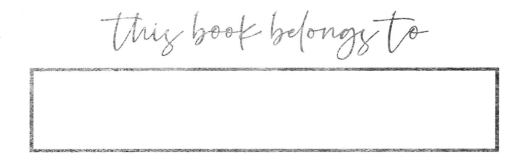

this book belongs to

For our divine daughters.

—Amber Corkin & Aubri Robinson

Text © 2021 Amber Corkin and Aubri Robinson
Artwork © 2021 Brooke Bowen, Brooklynne Noe, Ellie Osborne, Emily Shay Tueller, Heather Ruttan, Justine Peterson, Samantha Long, and Sarah Hawkes

ISBN 13: 978-1-4621-4041-1

Library of Congress Control Number: 2021934712

Published by CFI, an imprint of Cedar Fort, Inc.
2373 W. 700 S., Springville, UT 84663
Distributed by Cedar Fort, Inc., www.cedarfort.com

Cover and interior layout by Shawnda T. Craig
Cover design © 2021 Cedar Fort, Inc.

Printed in Colombia

10 9 8 7 6 5 4 3 2 1

DEAR DIVINE
Daughter

INSPIRING STORIES
OF BIBLE *Women*

written by
AMBER CORKIN & AUBRI ROBINSON

CFI • An imprint of Cedar Fort, Inc. • Springville, Utah

contents

artwork

introduction

T his book contains thirty-four inspiring and true stories of women in the Bible, each distinguished by an adjective capturing a divine characteristic she exemplifies. The last story in the book is for you to fill in your own name, story, and picture.

We hope as you read *Dear Divine Daughter: Inspiring Stories of Bible Women*, you will understand a few key truths: You are a daughter of God, the scriptures are home to many incredible women with a variety of divine characteristics, and you too can develop your own divine attributes.

ABIGAIL

peacemaking

Once upon a time there was a beautiful woman named Abigail. She was married to Nabal, a rich but rude man. They lived in a town called Maon and owned three thousand sheep and one thousand goats.

One day an army of soldiers passed through Maon, exhausted and starving from their travels. Their captain, David, had often helped Nabal by having his men form a wall of protection around the sheep and shepherds to guard them from danger. Thinking Nabal would now be kind in return, David sent a few men to politely ask for food, but Nabal rudely refused. He loudly criticized David and selfishly turned the men away empty-handed.

When his men returned and told David what had happened, David was offended and angry. He wanted revenge. After fastening his sword to his belt, David marched toward Nabal's home. Four hundred of his men loyally grabbed their swords and followed after him.

A servant saw what was happening and ran to warn Abigail. Quickly, without Nabal knowing, Abigail gathered heaps of food, including two hundred loaves of bread, two hundred fig cakes, and five sheep. She loaded the food onto donkeys and rode off to find David.

When Abigail saw David, she jumped off her donkey and bowed herself before him. Putting her face to the ground, Abigail begged David to forgive Nabal and not harm him. Softened by her plea, David realized he had overreacted. He called Abigail blessed, thanked her for being a peacemaker, and gratefully accepted her generous offering of food.

With peace restored, Abigail went home. A few days later, Nabal fell ill and died. When David heard the news, he asked Abigail to marry him. She accepted his proposal and they were married.

Dear divine daughter, how can you be a peacemaker?

1 Samuel 25:2-42

ANNA

holy

Once upon a time there was a holy woman named Anna. She had been married seven years when, sadly, her husband died. For the next eighty-four years, she lived alone as a widow.

Anna was devoted to the Lord and always stayed close to the temple. In fact, Anna was a prophetess. Even when she was over one hundred years old, Anna fasted and prayed to God night and day in the temple.

One day at the Temple of Jerusalem, in the Court of the Women, Anna saw a woman and man holding a new baby. Because Anna lived a consecrated life and was in tune with the Spirit, she immediately knew the baby was Jesus, the Savior.

When she saw Jesus, Anna thanked God and prophesied of Jesus's purpose and special mission on Earth. She testified of Him to everyone in Jerusalem who looked for redemption and desired to be saved from their sins.

Dear divine daughter, how can you be more holy?

Luke 2:36–38

DEBORAH

just

Once upon a time there was a wise woman named Deborah. Not only was Deborah a prophetess, she was also a righteous judge over Israel. People traveled to Deborah seeking her fair judgment.

Deborah was concerned about her people, the Israelites. An enemy king, Jabin, had reigned over them for twenty years with his powerful army.

Believing it was just and fair for the Israelites to be free, Deborah sent for a warrior named Barak. She told Barak that God had a mission for him. With an army of ten thousand men, Barak was to go to Mount Tabor to battle King Jabin's army. Deborah prophesied God would help Barak be victorious. She also prophesied a woman would ultimately defeat King Jabin's cruel army captain, Sisera. Barak was scared and said he would only go if Deborah came with him. So, she did.

When Sisera received news that Barak's army had come to battle at Mount Tabor, he gathered his powerful army, including nine hundred iron chariots, and went to fight Barak.

On the day of the battle, Deborah came to encourage Barak. She told him to rise up and fight for what was morally right. She reminded him that God would help him defeat his enemy. Barak followed Deborah's counsel and led his men into battle.

As they fought, Sisera and his army panicked. Flustered, Sisera jumped off his chariot and ran away, leaving his entire army to fall by the sword. Just as Deborah had prophesied, Barak was victorious, and Sisera was soon killed by a woman named Jael.

The Israelites continued to fight against the enemy king Jabin until he was destroyed. Deborah was such a big part of the Israelites' victory that a song was written about her celebrating that historic event.

Dear divine daughter, how can you be more just?

Judges 4; Judges 5:1–15

THE DEBTOR WIDOW
trusting

Once upon a time there lived a widow and her two sons. Her husband had been a righteous man who served the prophet Elisha.

One day, a creditor came to the widow's home to collect money she owed, but this widow was poor and could not pay him. All she had in her home was one pot of oil. Needing some form of payment, the creditor said he would take her sons as slaves in place of the money. Desperate, the widow found Elisha and cried for his help.

After listening to the widow's plea, Elisha told her to borrow empty pots from all her neighbors. She was then counseled to pour the oil from her own pot into all the borrowed pots.

The widow trusted the prophet and did as she was told. As she filled each borrowed pot to the brim, her oil miraculously multiplied, and her own pot never ran out.

The widow again found Elisha and told him of the miracle. Elisha instructed her to sell some of the oil to pay off her debts. The once-desperate widow and her sons lived off the remaining oil, and her sons were saved from bondage.

Dear divine daughter, how can you put your trust in God?

ELISABETH

hopeful

Once upon a time there was a righteous woman named Elisabeth. She lived near Jerusalem with her husband, Zacharias. For many years, Elisabeth and Zacharias had prayed for a child, but one had never come. Yet even after Elisabeth grew too old to become pregnant, she remained hopeful.

One day, an angel appeared to Zacharias as he worked in the temple. The angel told him Elisabeth would have a baby who would become a prophet and help others come to Christ. He and Elisabeth were to name their baby John.

The angel's prophecy came true. Even in her old age, Elisabeth miraculously became pregnant. Meanwhile, the same angel appeared to her cousin Mary, who would later become the mother of Jesus. The angel told Mary about Elisabeth's miraculous pregnancy and reminded Mary that with God's help, anything is possible.

Elisabeth's time to have her baby came, and she bore a son. All her neighbors and family celebrated with Elisabeth, knowing that, finally, God had blessed her with the child she hoped for.

When the baby was eight days old, he was circumcised and given a name. People tried to call him Zacharias after his father, but Elisabeth corrected them. She said his name would be John, as the angel had instructed. Despite the people's resistance, Elisabeth insisted.

Elisabeth nurtured John as he grew and became spiritually strong. When John was grown, he fulfilled his role in preparing the people to receive Jesus Christ, just as the angel had prophesied. Jesus called John the greatest of all men.

Dear divine daughter, how can you be more hopeful?

Luke 1:5–80; Luke 7:28

ESTHER
brave

Once upon a time there was an orphan named Esther. After her parents died, Esther's cousin Mordecai, who was a loyal servant to the king, cared for her.

Esther lived in a kingdom ruled by the powerful King Ahasuerus. One day he ordered all the fair maidens in the land to come before him. His favorite would be crowned queen. Esther went, but because she was Jewish and King Ahasuerus was not, she kept her religion a secret. The king favored Esther, who was very beautiful, and crowned her queen.

Meanwhile, all the king's servants bowed to his right-hand man, Haman. Mordecai would not, because he only worshipped God. This made Haman angry. He came up with an evil plan to get rid of Mordecai, urging the king to decree that every Jew be put to death.

Mordecai asked Esther to go before the king and beg for her people's lives. Esther knew this would be dangerous. Anyone who approached the king without being summoned could be put to death. Esther courageously said that if she died, so be it.

Esther asked Mordecai to gather the Jews and fast on her behalf. For three days and nights, they fasted and prayed. Then Esther bravely went before the king.

Instead of putting her to death, King Ahasuerus held out his golden scepter and allowed her to approach and speak. Esther asked if he and Haman could come to a banquet she had prepared.

At the banquet, Esther revealed her Jewish heritage to the king and asked for her life and the lives of her people to be spared. King Ahasuerus was angry at Haman, ordered he be put to death, and reversed the decree against the Jews.

Jews throughout the land rejoiced. To this day they still celebrate brave Queen Esther.

Dear divine daughter, how can you be brave?

Esther 2–4; Esther 5:1–8; Esther 7; Esther 8:1–8; Esther 9:26–32

HAGAR
obedient

Once upon a time there was an Egyptian slave named Hagar. She worked for Sarah, the wife of Abraham, but was treated poorly.

One day, Hagar ran away, but God told her to return home and again serve Sarah as a slave. He promised Hagar many descendants and told her she was already pregnant with a son named Ishmael. Obeying the Lord, Hagar returned. As promised, Hagar gave birth to a baby boy.

Years later, Hagar and Ishmael were banished from their home into the desert with only a bottle of water and some bread. They wandered in the dry desert and soon ran out of water, leaving them extremely thirsty. After laying Ishmael under a bush, Hagar turned and walked away. She did not want to watch her son die of thirst.

Crying, Hagar desperately prayed. God told her to not fear. After instructing Hagar to return to Ishmael, lift him up, and hold him in her hands, God promised a great nation would descend from Ishmael. Then God opened Hagar's eyes and she saw a well of water. She filled her bottle with water from the well, returned to Ishmael, and gave him water to drink.

As her son grew, God was with him. Ishmael became the father of a great nation, just as God had promised Hagar.

Dear divine daughter, how can you be more obedient to God?

Genesis 16; Genesis 17:20; Genesis 21:9–21; Genesis 25:12–18

HANNAH
honorable

Once upon a time there was a woman named Hannah. She was married to a man named Elkanah who loved her deeply, but they could not have children.

Every year Hannah and Elkanah went to the temple to worship and make a sacrifice. Elkanah always honored Hannah by giving her a notable portion of food at the yearly feast. One year at the feast, Hannah was teased for not having children. She wept and could not eat. Concerned, Elkanah asked Hannah why she was crying and tenderly comforted her.

After the feast, Hannah was overcome with grief. She wept and prayed to God for help. Hannah vowed to God that if He would give her a son, she would dedicate her son's life to Him.

A priest named Eli watched Hannah's silent prayer and asked her what was wrong. Hannah explained she had poured her soul out to God in prayer. Eli told her to go in peace because God would grant her righteous petition. Hannah went away happy.

Later, Hannah gave birth to a son and named him Samuel. When he was still very young, Hannah brought Samuel to Eli in the temple. Keeping her promise to God, she honorably gave Samuel to Him. From then on, Samuel worshipped and worked in the temple.

Every year when Hannah went to the temple, she brought Samuel a coat she had made for him. Although Hannah was separated from her son, she prayed to God and rejoiced, praising God for lifting her up and strengthening her.

Because Hannah was so honorable in keeping her promise, God blessed her with more children. She gave birth to three more sons and two daughters.

Dear divine daughter, how can you be honorable and keep your promises?

1 Samuel 1; 1 Samuel 2:1–11, 18–21

HULDAH

learned

Once upon a time there was a prophetess named Huldah who lived in an area of Jerusalem known as the college. Most people in her day could not read, and it was especially rare among women. Huldah, however, had studied and learned to read.

At the time, the king of Jerusalem was a righteous man named Josiah who began repairing the rundown temple. While the temple was under construction, a priest found a book that contained God's law given by Moses. The book was brought to King Josiah and read aloud by his scribe.

Upon hearing the words, King Josiah tore his clothes in grief. He was worried the Lord would be angry because the previous generation had been so wicked.

King Josiah ordered the priest and scribe to go ask the Lord about the book. The men also went to find Huldah because they wanted her insight as a prophetess.

Huldah read the book and told them what King Josiah feared was true. The Lord would indeed bring evil upon Jerusalem because of its past wickedness and idol worship. She confirmed the book was the word of God and that everything described in the book would happen.

Despite God's anger with the wicked people, Huldah had good news to share: Pleased with King Josiah, God promised to not do anything to Jerusalem as long as he was still alive. God would reward King Josiah's righteousness by letting him live in peace.

The priest and scribe respected Huldah and believed her prophecy. In addition to being a smart, literate woman, she had recognized the book as God's word. The priest and scribe told King Josiah what Huldah had said. Because of her words, King Josiah made a covenant to keep God's commandments with all his heart and soul.

Dear divine daughter, how can you be more learned?

18

2 Kings 22; 2 Kings 23:1-3

JEHOSHEBA

pioneering

Once upon a time there was a pioneering woman named Jehosheba. Her wicked grandmother and mother did not set a good example for her. Instead of following in their footsteps, Jehosheba chose to be righteous. She married a priest and spent her life serving God and working in the temple.

One day, Jehosheba found herself in a sticky situation. Her half-brother was the king, and when he died their mother, Athaliah, wanted to be queen. Athaliah plotted a murderous scheme to kill every member of the royal family who could take the throne from her.

When Athaliah began putting people to death, Jehosheba ran and hid her baby nephew, Joash, in the temple. Athaliah did not notice that Joash was missing among the dead, and Jehosheba kept him hidden in the temple for six years while Athaliah ruled on the throne.

When Joash was seven years old, he came out of hiding. The guards recognized Joash as their rightful ruler and encircled him, protecting him with their weapons. Joash was anointed king of Judah in front of the people, who clapped their hands and thanked God.

When Athaliah heard the noise coming from the temple, she went to investigate. She saw the young king and realized what was happening. Tearing her clothes in rage and despair, Athaliah yelled and accused Joash of treason. The captains and officers forced her out of the temple, and she was put to death.

Following Jehosheba's example, the young King Joash turned from his wicked family's ways and chose to be righteous. As King Joash reigned on the throne, Jehosheba and all the people rejoiced, and there was peace in the land.

Dear divine daughter, how can you be pioneering and choose to be different in good ways?

2 Kings 11; 2 Chronicles 22:10–12

JOANNA

dependable

Once upon a time there was a woman named Joanna who was possessed by evil spirits and burdened with diseases. She lived during the time of Christ and was miraculously healed of these afflictions.

Joanna became a dependable disciple of Jesus Christ. While He traveled throughout every city and village preaching, Joanna faithfully traveled with Him. As the wife of an important court official, Joanna used her resources to help take care of Jesus and His disciples.

When Joanna learned that Jesus would die, she cried and mourned. She stood watching as Jesus selflessly hung on the cross.

After Christ's death, Joanna continued to be dependable. When Joanna approached the burial tomb to anoint Christ's body with spices and ointments she had lovingly prepared, she was surprised to see the stone covering the tomb entrance had been rolled away. Christ's body was gone.

As Joanna wondered what had happened to His body, two angels suddenly appeared. Frightened, she bowed down to the ground, but the angels comforted Joanna. They told her Jesus had risen from the dead. Joanna then remembered what Jesus had said would happen after His death: He would live again.

Joanna ran to tell the Apostles what had happened. Most thought her story was made up, but Peter believed her. He ran to the tomb and saw what Joanna had seen and described. Jesus had risen!

Dear divine daughter, how can you be more dependable in your service to God?

Luke 8:1-3; Luke 24:1-12, 22-24

JOCHEBED
creative

Once upon a time there was a woman named Jochebed who lived during difficult times. When she was expecting her third child, the ruler of the land, Pharaoh, ordered that every Hebrew baby boy throughout Egypt should be thrown into the river and drowned.

Jochebed gave birth to a son. Fearing for his life, she hid him from Pharaoh's men. After three months, Jochebed could no longer keep him hidden and safe, so she came up with a creative plan.

Jochebed took bulrushes from the water's edge and wove the long, grass-like stems together to make a basket. Knowing that water could seep through the woven bulrushes, Jochebed smeared it with slime and pitch. The basket exterior then hardened, creating a safe and dry vessel.

Tucking her son into the basket, Jochebed laid it among the reeds at the edge of the river and asked her daughter to follow the basket to see where it went.

Pharaoh's daughter, the princess, had come to the river to bathe and found the basket. She took compassion on the crying baby inside. Jochebed's daughter watched this happen and approached the princess, offering to find a Hebrew woman who could nurse the baby. She ran and brought Jochebed. The princess, not knowing Jochebed was the baby's mother, let her feed and care for the child as he grew.

Because of Jochebed's creative thinking, the boy's life was spared. Her son was named Moses, grew up in the palace, and later became an influential prophet who freed his people from slavery.

Dear divine daughter, how can you use your creativity to do good things?

Exodus 2:1–10; Exodus 6:20; Numbers 26:59; Hebrews 11:23–27

THE LITTLE MAID
virtuous

Once upon a time there was a little Hebrew girl in the land of Israel. She lived during a time of war, when the Syrians were fighting against her people.

The Syrians, led by a powerful captain, Naaman, won the war. Before leaving Israel to return home, the Syrians took the little Hebrew girl captive. They brought her back to Syria, where she became a servant to Naaman's wife. The little maid looked after her new mistress's needs, waiting on her and obeying her orders.

Because Naaman had won the war, he was considered to be a man of courage. But even though he was a fearless leader in the face of danger, Naaman had a physical weakness: He suffered from a painful skin disease called leprosy.

Despite Naaman's role in defeating her people, the little maid felt it was her moral duty to help him. She told her mistress of a prophet, Elisha, from her home in Israel who could heal Naaman. The news reached the ears of the king of Syria, who sent Naaman to Israel. With his horses and chariot, Naaman made his way to Elisha's door and was cleansed of his leprosy.

Because of the little maid's high moral standards in helping her enemy captor, Naaman returned home healed.

Dear divine daughter, how can you be virtuous and show high moral standards?

2 Kings 5:1–14

LYDIA
influential

Once upon a time there was a righteous woman named Lydia who sold purple dye for a living. Purple dye was expensive, so she was likely a wealthy, powerful, and influential woman with a successful career.

Though she was originally from Thyatira, Lydia had moved to a new city called Philippi. After she moved, the Apostles Paul and Silas visited Philippi to do missionary work. One day, Lydia and a group of women went to a nearby riverbank to hear Paul and Silas preach.

As Lydia sat listening to Paul speak, the Lord opened her heart. She believed his words and chose to follow what he taught. Lydia made the decision to be baptized. Her whole household was influenced by her good example, and they all chose to be baptized as well.

Hoping Paul and Silas saw her as a faithful disciple of Christ, Lydia asked them to come live in her home. They agreed, and Lydia housed the Apostles while they continued their missionary work in Philippi.

Dear divine daughter, how can you be a righteous influence on others?

Acts 16:12–15, 40

MARTHA

caring

Once upon a time there was a woman named Martha who lived in a small village called Bethany with her siblings, Lazarus and Mary. Martha was a faithful disciple of Jesus, and He loved her very much.

One day Jesus came to visit, and Martha gladly welcomed Him into her home. Both Martha and Mary sat at Jesus's feet and listened as He taught. Having a kind and caring heart, Martha eventually got up and began serving Jesus, making sure He was well taken care of.

A while later, when Jesus was in another city, Lazarus became very sick. Worried about their brother, Martha and Mary sent a message to Jesus, who they knew could heal him. After a couple of days, Jesus began His journey toward their home in Bethany, but before He could get there, Lazarus died. Martha mourned his death but continued to anticipate Jesus's arrival.

As soon as Martha heard Jesus was near, she went to meet Him. Martha told Jesus that if He had been there sooner, Lazarus would not have died. She knew, however, that Jesus was the Son of God and could perform any miracle He desired. They went to Lazarus's grave and Jesus raised him from the dead.

Later, during the last week before Jesus's death, He again visited Martha's home. As a loving disciple, she once again welcomed Jesus and cared for Him.

Dear divine daughter, how can you be more caring?

Luke 10:38–42; John 11:1–44; John 12:1–2

MARY MAGDALENE
devoted

Once upon a time there was a woman in the seaside village of Magdala who was possessed by seven evil spirits. Her name was Mary Magdalene.

Jesus saw Mary and had compassion on her. He cast out the evil spirits, and Mary became one of Jesus's closest friends and a devoted disciple. Even at the end of Jesus's life, she stood nearby, supporting Him as He was crucified on the cross.

When Mary went to anoint the body of Jesus in His burial tomb, she was surprised to discover He was gone. After she ran to tell two of Jesus's Apostles that His body was missing, they came and saw for themselves what Mary had described. The two Apostles left, but Mary remained.

Devastated that someone would steal the body of her friend and Savior, Mary sat mourning beside the tomb. Suddenly, two angels dressed in pure white appeared. They asked Mary why she was crying and she explained her tears.

Just then, the resurrected Savior appeared behind her. Jesus asked why she wept and for whom she was looking. Perhaps because of all her tears, Mary did not recognize Jesus when He spoke. She thought He was the gardener and asked if He knew where Jesus's body had been taken.

Uttering one word that changed Mary's tears of sorrow into tears of joy, Jesus said, "Mary." Now recognizing Him, Mary reached out for Jesus and replied, "Master." Jesus asked Mary to go tell the disciples that He had yet to ascend to God. Loyally running to tell the news, Mary went and shared her sacred experience and testimony.

Dear divine daughter, how can you be a more devoted disciple?

Luke 8:1–3; Luke 24:1–12; Matthew 27:55–61; Matthew 28:1–10;
Mark 15:39–47; Mark 16:1–11; John 20:1–18

MARY, MOTHER OF JESUS

receptive

Once upon a time there was a beautiful young woman named Mary. She was engaged to a carpenter named Joseph.

One day an angel appeared to Mary, calling her highly favored and blessed among women. He said Mary would become pregnant and give birth to the Son of God. She was to name Him Jesus. Mary was receptive, willing to be God's servant and do anything God asked of her.

When Mary was about to give birth, she and Joseph traveled nearly one hundred miles from Nazareth to Joseph's hometown of Bethlehem to be taxed. When they arrived they searched for somewhere to stay and have the baby, but there was no room at the inn.

Instead they found shelter in a humble stable where Mary gave birth to the Savior of the world. She tenderly wrapped Him in swaddling clothes and laid Him in a manger. Shepherds came to worship Jesus and then spread the wonderful news of His birth abroad. Mary, however, privately pondered on the sacred experience.

Later, Mary brought baby Jesus to the temple. A prophet testified of Jesus's mission and confirmed Mary's divine role as His mother, though he warned she would face great heartache because of it. Mary received his words and marveled at the prophecy.

When Jesus was twelve, his family took their yearly trip to the Feast of the Passover. On their way home, Mary realized Jesus was missing. She and Joseph searched for days and finally found Jesus at the temple. He told them He was going about His Father's business. Mary did not understand this, but she was open-minded and pondered His words.

After years of fulfilling her special role as Jesus's mother, Mary stood watching and mourning as her son suffered and died on the cross.

Dear divine daughter, how can you be more receptive to God, the Holy Ghost, and others?

Luke 1:26–38; Luke 2; John 19:25–27

MARY OF BETHANY
humble

Once upon a time there lived a disciple named Mary who was often found humbly kneeling at the feet of Jesus.

One day Jesus visited Mary's home, where she sat on the ground listening to Him teach. Despite busy tasks being done around them by others in her home, Mary stayed focused on His wise words. When her sister asked Mary for help serving the guests, Jesus supported Mary's decision to stay and learn at His feet.

Later, Mary's brother died. Mourning, she sat in her home among supportive friends. Privately approaching Mary so as not to draw attention, her sister told Mary that Jesus had come and wanted to see her. Mary quickly arose and went to Jesus. She humbly fell at His feet in tears, knowing He could have saved her brother. Jesus loved Mary very much. When she wept, Jesus wept with her. Then He went to her brother's grave and miraculously raised him from the dead.

During Jesus's last week on earth, He again visited Mary's home. She brought expensive ointment and anointed His feet with the oil, reverently wiping them with her hair. One of Jesus's disciples asked why Mary was wasting the expensive ointment instead of selling it to give the money to the poor. Jesus said to leave her be. There would always be poor people to help, but He would not always be with them. Mary humbly honored Him.

Dear divine daughter, how can you be more humble?

Luke 10:38-42; John 11:1-45; John 12:1-8

MICHAL

selfless

Once upon a time there was a princess named Michal who was the daughter of King Saul. She was in love with a heroic warrior named David.

King Saul was jealous of David's success and wanted him gone. He agreed to Michal and David's marriage only if David would go to war and defeat one hundred men from the Philistine army. He had hoped David would die in the process, but to King Saul's astonishment, David defeated two hundred Philistine men and returned home victorious. David and Michal were soon married.

Now even more jealous of David's fame, King Saul again secretly plotted against him. One night he threw a javelin at David but missed, hitting the wall instead. Afraid for his life, David fled from the king and ran home to Michal. King Saul sent messengers to watch Michal's house and capture David the next morning.

Michal told David if he did not escape that night, he would surely die the next day. Though she knew the king would be furious with her, Michal selflessly helped David climb out the window and escape with his life. She then created a diversion to buy David more time, arranging a pillow and cloth on David's bed to make it look like he was still sleeping there. When the king's messengers came to capture David the next morning, Michal convinced them he was sick in bed and they left empty-handed.

King Saul sent messengers a second time with orders to bring David even if they had to bring him in bed. This time the messengers discovered Michal's pile of cloth and the pillow. David was nowhere to be found because Michal risked her own life to save him.

Dear divine daughter, how can you be more selfless and help others in their time of need?

1 Samuel 18:20–30; 1 Samuel 19:8–18

MIRIAM
confident

Once upon a time there was a young Hebrew slave named Miriam. When the wicked king Pharaoh ordered all the Hebrew baby boys to be thrown into the Nile River, Miriam had a brand-new baby brother, Moses, whom she wanted to protect.

Knowing Moses would not be safe with them, Miriam's mom put Moses into a basket and placed it among reeds at the river's edge. Although it pained them, giving him up was the only way to save his life. Miriam stayed to watch the basket, waiting to see what would unfold.

Soon, Pharaoh's daughter came to the riverbank to bathe. She heard a baby crying and discovered the basket among the reeds. Opening it, the princess found Moses inside.

Although Miriam was a lowly Hebrew slave, she confidently approached the princess. Knowing she would need someone to feed the baby, Miriam spoke up and asked if she could find a Hebrew woman to nurse the child. The princess accepted Miriam's assertive offer. Delighted, Miriam quickly ran and brought her mother, who served as Moses's nurse. Miriam was then able to watch her brother grow and become an influential prophet.

Later in her life Miriam became a confident leader and prophetess who received revelation and direction from God. When the Israelites were freed from bondage, Miriam recognized God's hand in their escape from Pharaoh. She took a tambourine and led all the women in singing, dancing, and glorifying God.

Dear divine daughter, how can you be more confident?

Numbers 26:59; Exodus 2:1–10; Exodus 15:20–21; Micah 6:4

NAOMI

long-suffering

Once upon a time there was a righteous woman named Naomi from the city of Bethlehem. When there was a famine in the land, Naomi and her husband and two sons moved to Moab in search of more food.

Tragedy soon fell on their household. Naomi's husband died, leaving her a widow and her sons fatherless. Within ten years, both of her sons also died. Feeling she had nothing left to offer her sons' wives, Orpah and Ruth, Naomi told them to return to their own mothers.

Naomi decided to move back to Bethlehem, kissed her daughters-in-law, and bid them farewell, but Ruth refused to let Naomi leave alone. She loved Naomi and said that wherever Naomi went, she would go too.

When they arrived in Bethlehem, Naomi's friends saw her and called out her name. Devastated by the death of her husband and sons, however, Naomi said that her name, which means "pleasantness," should be changed to "Mara," which means "sorrow." Though she was understandably saddened by her hardships, Naomi was not angry with God. She remained long-suffering, righteously enduring her many trials.

Eventually, happiness came. Naomi was given food by a wealthy and kind man whom she later encouraged Ruth to marry. Soon, Naomi was blessed with a grandson who brought her much comfort and joy.

Dear divine daughter, how can you be more long-suffering and endure hard things?

Ruth 1; Ruth 2:1–3, 18–23; Ruth 3:1–6, 16–18; Ruth 4:3–17

THE POOR WIDOW
generous

Once upon a time there was a widow who was devoted to God and extremely poor. She lived in Jerusalem at the same time as Jesus.

One day the widow went to the temple to visit the treasury, an area in the courtyard of the temple where women and men could pay tithes and offerings to God. The widow approached the treasury and prepared to make her donation.

Ahead of her, rich men threw in a great deal of money, loudly showing off their significant wealth and contributions. Humbly, the widow pulled out just two mites and dropped them in. At the time, a mite was the smallest Jewish coin, worth less than half a penny.

Jesus sat against the treasury, watching people as they threw in their money. He saw the widow give her two mites and was pleased with her, recognizing the true value of what she gave.

Gathering His disciples around Him, Jesus described what had happened and explained that the widow had given more than anyone else. The others had put in a lot of money but kept much more for themselves. The widow had put in all the money she possessed. With literally nothing left to offer, she had generously given all she had to God.

Dear divine daughter, how can you be more generous to God and others?

Mark 12:41-44; Luke 21:1-4

PUAH AND SHIPHRAH

God-fearing

Once upon a time there were two Hebrew women named Puah and Shiphrah who lived in Israel. Midwives by trade, they helped support women in childbirth. Puah and Shiphrah stayed busy because of all the babies being born.

Meanwhile, an evil king of Egypt ruled over the Israelites. Because so many Israelites were being born and the people were filling the land, the king feared they were becoming more powerful than he and might one day overthrow him.

To weaken the Israelites, the king forced them to do backbreaking labor, constructing large buildings and slaving away in the fields. Despite their exhaustion, the harder the Israelites worked, the more children they had.

Alarmed by his failed attempt to weaken them, the king devised an even more wicked plan. He gave Puah and Shiphrah an order: From now on, if a Hebrew baby boy was born, they were to kill the infant. If the baby was a girl, they could let her live.

Although the king was powerful, Puah and Shiphrah feared God more than the evil king. Bravely disobeying the king's command, they secretly saved the baby boys, allowing them to live.

The king discovered what Puah and Shiphrah were doing and demanded they explain themselves. To trick the king, Puah and Shiphrah said the babies were being born so quickly they could not reach the mothers in time to intervene.

God was pleased with Puah and Shiphrah for risking their lives to save the baby boys, so He blessed Puah and Shiphrah with descendants as a reward for their righteousness.

Because Puah and Shiphrah foiled the king's plan, the Israelites continued to multiply and became a mighty people. Eventually, they were freed from the Egyptians and bondage.

Dear divine daughter, how can you be more God-fearing?

Exodus 1:7-21

RAHAB
action-oriented

Once upon a time there was a woman named Rahab who lived in Jericho, a city full of people who did not believe in God. Her home was built on the city wall.

One day God commanded Joshua, a righteous Israelite leader, to capture Jericho. Joshua sent two men to spy on Jericho and scope out the land. Slipping into the city by night, the spies came to Rahab's home and asked if they could stay there. She invited them in.

When the king of Jericho was told that spies had taken shelter in Rahab's home, he sent messengers ordering her to turn them in. But Rahab felt that God wanted her to help the spies, so she acted quickly and hid them on her roof behind stalks of flax.

Rahab told the messengers she had not known the men were spies and said they had already left through the city gate. She encouraged the messengers to hurry and chase after the spies in order to capture them. Tricked by Rahab's story, the messengers rushed out the city gate.

Rahab returned to the roof and assured the spies that God would help their people conquer Jericho. She pleaded with them to not hurt her family when Jericho was captured, and the spies agreed.

Rahab helped the spies escape by lowering a scarlet rope out her window for them to climb down. The spies asked Rahab to leave the rope tied to her window and told her that when their people came to capture the city, they would look for the rope and spare everyone in the house. Rahab faithfully followed their instructions, and she and her entire household were saved.

Dear divine daughter, how can you be more action-oriented and act on your faith?

Joshua 2; Joshua 6:1-5, 17, 22-25; Hebrews 11:31

REBEKAH

inspired

Once upon a time there was a beautiful damsel named Rebekah.

One day while Rebekah filled her pitcher with water from the well, a stranger approached her and asked for a drink. Rebekah not only gave him water; she also filled a trough for his camels and welcomed him into her family's home to rest and eat.

The man explained he was on a quest to find his master's son, Isaac, a wife. After stopping at the well, he had prayed that Isaac's future wife would offer him and his camels water. Rebekah was inspired and had answered his prayer.

Because she felt it was the right thing to do, Rebekah agreed to marry Isaac. Before she left, her family blessed her to have millions of descendants. Soon, the two were married, and Isaac loved Rebekah.

Despite her blessing, for a while Rebekah could not have children. When she finally became pregnant, she felt something happening in her womb and prayed to God for clarity. God revealed to her that she was pregnant with twins and that the older twin would serve the younger. Sure enough, Rebekah gave birth to twin boys, Esau and Jacob.

Years later, Isaac wanted to give Esau, the older twin, his inheritance. But remembering that God had said the older son should serve the younger son, Rebekah was inspired to intervene so that Isaac would give Jacob the inheritance instead. Knowing that Isaac was going blind, Rebekah disguised Jacob to feel and smell like his older brother. She tied goatskins around his arms and neck to make him feel hairy and dressed him in Esau's clothes. The plan worked. Thinking Jacob was Esau, Isaac blessed him to rule over his brother and nations, just as God had foretold.

Dear divine daughter, how can you become more inspired and receive revelation from God?

50

Genesis 24; Genesis 25:20-34; Genesis 27:5-29

THE REPENTANT WOMAN

repentant

Once upon a time there was a woman who lived in Galilee who was known as a sinner.

When she learned Jesus was attending a banquet at the home of Simon, a Pharisee, she retrieved her beautiful alabaster box filled with expensive ointment and carried it to Simon's house.

Standing behind Jesus while He sat at the table, the woman began to cry. She was deeply sorry for her sins. Reverently, the woman began to wash His feet with her tears and wipe them with her hair. She humbly kissed His feet and rubbed them with the expensive ointment she had brought.

When Simon saw the woman doing this, he disapproved. He thought if Jesus were really a prophet, He would know she was a sinner and not allow her to touch Him.

Perceiving Simon's thoughts, Jesus scolded him. Simon had not cared to wash His feet, but the woman had washed His feet with her tears and wiped them with her hair. Simon had not greeted Him with a kiss, but the woman had not stopped kissing His feet. Simon had not anointed Jesus's head with oil, but the woman had anointed even His feet with her precious oil.

Then, to Simon's surprise, Jesus declared that even though the woman's sins were many, she was forgiven because she deeply loved Him. Turning to the woman, Jesus tenderly said, "Thy sins are forgiven." He complimented her faith and told her she could go in peace.

Dear divine daughter, how can you be more repentant?

Luke 7:36-50

53

RHODA
persistent

Once upon a time there was a young girl named Rhoda who lived during a scary and uncertain time for Christians. King Herod had just killed the Apostle James, and the Apostle Peter had been cast into prison.

One night, Rhoda was faithfully praying with a group of people gathered in a large house in the city of Jerusalem. As Rhoda prayed, she heard a knock at the door of the gate.

Heading toward the gate, Rhoda recognized Peter's voice coming from outside. Because she thought Peter was still in prison, Rhoda was thrilled at the sound. In all her excitement, she forgot to open the gate for Peter before running back inside to tell everyone the good news.

No one believed Rhoda, because they also thought Peter was still bound in prison. They told her she was crazy, but Rhoda knew she had heard the voice of the Apostle and would not let them tell her otherwise. Knowing for certain it was Peter who had spoken to her through the gate, she insisted he really was outside. Yet even after she persisted, they wondered if she had perhaps seen Peter's ghost.

Finally, others also heard knocking at the gate. When they opened the door, they were amazed to see that Peter was indeed standing outside. What Rhoda had been telling them was true.

Dear divine daughter, how can you be more persistent despite opposition?

Acts 12:1–17

RUTH
loyal

Once upon a time there was a young widow named Ruth. Though she was heartbroken by the recent death of her husband, Ruth had compassion on her mother-in-law, Naomi, who had lost her husband and two sons.

When Naomi told her daughters-in-law, Ruth and Orpah, she was moving back to Bethlehem, Ruth and Orpah followed her. But Naomi had nothing left to offer them and told them to return to their mothers' homes. Despite Ruth and Orpah's protests and tears, Naomi insisted. Eventually, Orpah kissed Naomi goodbye and left, but Ruth refused to go.

Ruth declared that wherever Naomi would live, she would live too. Naomi's people would become her people. Naomi's God would become her God. Only death could part them. Seeing Ruth's firm commitment to her, Naomi conceded, and they journeyed together.

The women arrived in Bethlehem at the beginning of the barley harvest. Ruth went to the fields owned by a wealthy man named Boaz to find food. She gathered bits of barley his servants had left behind.

Boaz knew what Ruth had sacrificed to care for Naomi and was impressed by her loyalty. Boaz told Ruth she was always welcome in his fields and asked his servants to leave extra food for her. For the rest of the barley season, Ruth lived with Naomi and worked in the fields to provide for their needs.

Knowing Boaz was a good man, Naomi encouraged Ruth to propose to him. That night, Ruth asked Boaz for his hand in marriage. Boaz complimented her unwavering kindness and virtue and willingly agreed to marry her.

After they were wed, Ruth gave birth to a son, and Naomi helped care for the boy. Ruth's deep love for Naomi, which was said to be greater than the love of seven sons, never wavered.

Dear divine daughter, how can you be more loyal?

Ruth 1–4

THE SAMARITAN WOMAN AT THE WELL

missionary—minded

Once upon a time there lived a Samaritan woman in a city called Sychar.

One day when she went to fetch water from the well, she saw a man, weary from a long journey, sitting on the well to rest. He turned to the woman and asked her for some water to drink. The woman, seeing that He was a Jew, was shocked He had addressed her. Jews did not usually talk to Samaritans, because their people were long-time enemies.

The man told the woman He had water that would make her never thirst again. Intrigued at the idea of never having to come to the well again, the woman asked for some of this water. As they talked He shared details of her life a stranger could never know, so she assumed He must be a prophet.

As they discussed spiritual things, the woman shared her testimony of Jesus with the man, saying she knew Jesus would come and teach truth. Then, to her amazement, the man revealed that He was Jesus.

Jumping up and leaving her water pot behind, the woman ran to the city. She spread the news that Jesus was at the well and invited everyone to come see Him for themselves. Motivated by her passionate testimony, many came to Jesus.

After He taught the Samaritans from the city, they begged Him to stay with them a while longer. Jesus willingly stayed for two more days, teaching them. Those who heard Him preach gained a sure testimony of Jesus for themselves.

Dear divine daughter, how can you be a better missionary and invite others to come unto Jesus?

John 4:6–30, 39–42

THE SHUNAMMITE WOMAN

problem—solving

Once upon a time there was a woman who lived in Shunem with her husband.

The prophet Elisha often passed by their home as he worked throughout the city. Seeing an opportunity to help, the woman made a bedroom for Elisha with a bed, table, stool, and candlestick. The next time he walked by, she invited him in to rest.

Grateful, Elisha asked what the woman wanted in return for her thoughtfulness. Although she asked for nothing, Elisha discovered she had no child. As a reward for her kindness, he said she would be blessed with a baby boy. Soon enough, the woman gave birth to a son.

Years later, her son injured his head while working in the fields. Cradling her only child on her lap, the woman held him as he died in her arms. Though she was devastated, the woman saddled a donkey and rode off to find Elisha.

When he heard what had happened, Elisha followed the woman to where her son's body lay. Elisha prayed to God, and the boy miraculously sneezed seven times and opened his eyes. When she saw her son was alive again, the woman fell down at Elisha's feet, thanking him.

Elisha respected this woman so much that, knowing a famine would soon come, he warned her to move away. The woman gathered her family and left the city, saving them from starvation.

When the famine ended seven years later, the woman and her family returned to Shunem, but there was still a problem. While they were gone, their property had been confiscated. Taking initiative, the woman asked the king for her property back. When he learned she was the one who had helped Elisha, the king willingly agreed to restore her home and land.

Dear divine daughter, how can you take initiative and find solutions to problems in your life?

2 Kings 4:8-37; 2 Kings 8:1-6

TABITHA

charitable

Once upon a time there was a woman named Tabitha who lived in the town of Joppa. Tabitha was known for her good works and deeds, as she was often found giving to the poor and lonely.

After Tabitha became sick and died, the people lovingly washed her body and laid her in an upstairs room of a house.

Peter, who was the prophet at the time, was visiting Saints throughout the land and came near Tabitha's hometown. The disciples in Joppa sent two men to Peter, asking him to hurry and come.

Sensing their urgency, Peter quickly came. When he arrived, Peter was brought upstairs to where Tabitha lay. All the widows stood beside Peter, crying. Showing him coats and clothes, they explained that Tabitha had generously made these gifts for them when she was alive.

After asking everyone to leave the room, Peter knelt down and prayed. Then, turning to Tabitha's body, he commanded her to arise. Miraculously, Tabitha opened her eyes, saw Peter, and sat up. Peter gave Tabitha his hand and helped her stand.

All the widows and Saints came and saw that Tabitha was alive again. The miracle was told throughout Joppa, and many people believed in God because of it.

Dear divine daughter, how can you be more charitable and help those in need?

Acts 9:32, 36–42

THE WIDOW OF ZAREPHATH
faithful

Once upon a time there was a poor widow who lived with her son in a small town called Zarephath.

One day the Lord instructed the prophet Elijah to journey to Zarephath and dwell there, telling him He had already commanded a widow there to care for him. Obeying the Lord, Elijah went to Zarephath and, as he approached the gate of the city, saw a widow gathering sticks. Elijah called to her and asked if she could fetch him some water to drink and a morsel of bread to eat.

The widow sadly confessed she had no food to give him. All she had left was a handful of flour in a barrel and a little oil in a jar. She said she was gathering sticks so she could return home and prepare her and her son's last meal. After eating their last bit of food, they would surely die of hunger.

Telling the widow not to fear, Elijah instructed her to go home and prepare the food as she had planned, but to make him a little cake first. Elijah promised God would not let their food run out.

Even though it meant sacrificing a precious portion of what she thought would be her last meal, the widow was faithful. She trusted God and followed the prophet Elijah's instructions. Just as Elijah promised, her flour and oil did not run out, and they all had enough to eat.

Dear divine daughter, how can you be more faithful?

1 Kings 17:8–16

THE WIFE OF PONTIUS PILATE

independent

Once upon a time there was a Roman woman who was married to the governor of Judea, Pontius Pilate. He had sat on the judgment seat, governing, for many years.

One day the chief priests tied up Jesus and brought Him before Pilate. Infuriated that Jesus performed miracles, went against tradition, and claimed to be the Son of God, they were jealous of His power and wanted Him to be killed. Pilate was in charge of deciding whether Jesus would live or die.

That same day, Pilate's wife had a vision of Jesus. The vision deeply affected her, and she suffered greatly from what she saw.

Pilate's wife sent her husband a message telling him Jesus was a just man. She asked Pilate to have nothing to do with Jesus's trial. Despite peer pressure to think otherwise, she knew Jesus was innocent and defended Him.

Pilate read his wife's message and agreed with her; there was no proof Jesus had done anything wrong. Meanwhile, many people had gathered and a riot broke out. Pressuring Pilate to destroy Jesus, they cried, "Let him be crucified!" When Pilate asked the people what evil Jesus had done to merit such harsh punishment, the crowd grew louder and more insistent.

Fearing the uproar but following his wife's open-minded advice, Pilate told the crowd he would not be responsible for Jesus's death. He stood before them and used water to symbolically wash his hands of the decision. He let the people decide Jesus's fate. Despite the vision Pilate's wife had and her testimony of His innocence, the crowd ultimately chose to crucify Jesus.

Dear divine daughter, how can you be more independent and stand for what is right instead of following the crowd?

Matthew 27:1-2, 11-26

THE WOMAN WITH AN ISSUE OF BLOOD

determined

Once upon a time there was a woman with a chronic illness. For twelve long years she had lost considerable amounts of blood and suffered every day. As was customary at that time, people thought she was unclean because of her condition. If they touched her, her bed, or anything she sat on, they were required to wash their clothes and bathe themselves. As a result, the woman was likely homeless and shunned from society.

Determined and desperate to find a cure, the woman went to many doctors and spent all her money in an effort to be healed, but no one could help her. Her illness only got worse.

One day the woman heard of Jesus and decided that if she could just touch His clothes, she would be made whole again. Seeing Jesus in a crowd and determined to reach Him, she struggled through the throng of people, reached out, and touched the hem of His garment. Immediately, the woman felt her bleeding stop. After years of searching, she had finally found healing.

Turning about, Jesus asked who had touched Him. His disciples were confused. There was a large crowd around Jesus, pushing into Him, so they wondered why He would ask. Even amid the crowd, Jesus had sensed a touch that had caused strength and power to leave Him.

Trembling with fear, the woman fell down at Jesus's feet. She confessed she had touched Him and said that doing so had healed her. Jesus comforted the woman and said her faith had made her whole. He told her to go in peace and live a life free of her illness.

Dear divine daughter, how can you be more determined when you face challenges?

Leviticus 15:25–30; Mark 5:24–34; Luke 8:43–48

YOUR NAME

your strongest divine characteristic

_____

Once upon a time _____

_____

_____

_____

_____

_____

_____

_____

_____

_____

_____

_____

_____

_____

_____

_____

_____

_____

(Your story)

Dear divine daughter, you are a beloved daughter of God. As an heiress of Him (Romans 8:17), you have unique and divine qualities. You have the limitless potential to be a mighty force for good in this world and in the eternities.

Draw a portrait or insert a photo of yourself here.

acknowledgments

We are deeply grateful to the many wonderful people assisting us with this passion project. Thank you. . .

To each of our husbands (Jake Corkin and Nathaniel Robinson) for your unwavering love, support, and belief in us. To our children (Johnny, Charlie Marie, and Vinnie and Zoey, Iris, and Skye) for being our "why" and for your patience while we tackled this almost-four-year project. To our mother (Jan LeBaron) and our sister (Ashley Black) for reading and re-reading versions of these stories and for fighting over our #1 fan spot. To our wonderful illustrators who jumped in with both feet, poured your hearts into your artwork, and truly brought these stories to life. To Mary Corkin and Elizabeth Maki for your helpful edits. To our friends, followers, and the many Kickstarter backers who generously invested in our project, blew us away with your support, and showed us how wanted this book truly is. And to Cedar Fort, Inc., for helping us get this book into the hands of more girls.

To all of you, a heart-felt thank you!

shining stars

Amelia LeBaron	Grace Sofia	Rebecca Leigh
April Louise	Iris Robinson	Reese Hull
Charlie Marie Corkin	Johnny Corkin	Skye Robinson
Chloé M	Juniper Skye	Tiffany Pyper
Emery Lindsey	Kaylee Bullock	Virginia Corkin
Evelyn Reber	Madeline Marie Holcomb	Zoey Robinson

authors

AMBER CORKIN

is a DIY home and food blogger with a penchant for doing, not just dreaming. She earned a business marketing degree from Brigham Young University and worked in women's fashion e-commerce before leaving to start her own business, The DIY Lighthouse. As a blogger, Amber has created content for household-name brands but also uses her platform to bring awareness to important topics like self-esteem and body image. Amber loves chasing lofty goals (like that one time she bicycled coast-to-coast across the U.S.) and enjoys exploring the outdoors with her husband, Jake, and their three young children.

AUBRI ROBINSON

is creative, friendly, and resilient. From her local church in Minnesota to the United Nations in Geneva, Switzerland, she has volunteered as an advocate for girls and women. Aubri has three cherished daughters and is madly in love with her husband, Nathaniel. A mother by day and an entrepreneur by night, Aubri owns a branding and website design company and has done creative work for top brands like Samsung®, Silk®, and Puddle Jumper®. As a type-1 diabetic with a passion for helping others, Aubri is pursuing graduate studies in healthcare.

artists

BROOKE BOWEN has loved to create since she was young. She attended BYU before continuing her art education independently. She now lives in the shadows of the mountains of Utah raising her four boys with an enthusiasm for creating.

BROOKLYNNE NOE is a Nashville-based illustrator and stay-at-home parent. Her journey through motherhood has inspired Brooklynne to portray stories of women's strength in her artwork. This will be her first book illustration work, and she couldn't be more excited!

ELLIE OSBORNE has been making art as long as she could hold a pencil. She's a fresh Illustration graduate who wants to make books for kids, especially about powerful historic figures—this project was a dream to be a part of!

EMILY SHAY TUELLER is a freelance illustrator based in Pleasant Grove, Utah. Emily has a unique approach in blending fine art, whimsy, and digitization. Her art has sold its way into thousands of homes throughout the world.

artists

HEATHER RUTTAN is a Canadian oil-pastel and digital artist. She has spent two years creating art focused on the Latter-day Saint doctrine of Heavenly Mother. She aims to increase representation in religious art, showing all ages, shapes, and colors of women as holy.

JUSTINE PETERSON is a mother, a teacher, and an artist. Painting in watercolors keeps her sane amongst the chaos of life and allows her to share her testimony when words are hard. Her husband is an artist as well, and their boys, Van Gogh, Rembrandt, and Raphael, are their greatest joy.

SAMANTHA LONG is an artist who loves patterns and whimsy. She creates her colorful images in oils with just a pinch of passion. She currently lives in American Fork, Utah with an empty guinea pig cage and an overflowing yarn stash.

SARAH HAWKES has been drawing since she could hold a pencil. For her, art is a way to bear her testimony. When she isn't making art, Sarah loves road trips, dark chocolate, Indian food, and listening to Adele.